COPING SKILLS WORKBOOK for Children

Child Edition

Written by:
Denise Folsom, LMHC, RPT, NBCC
The Legacy House

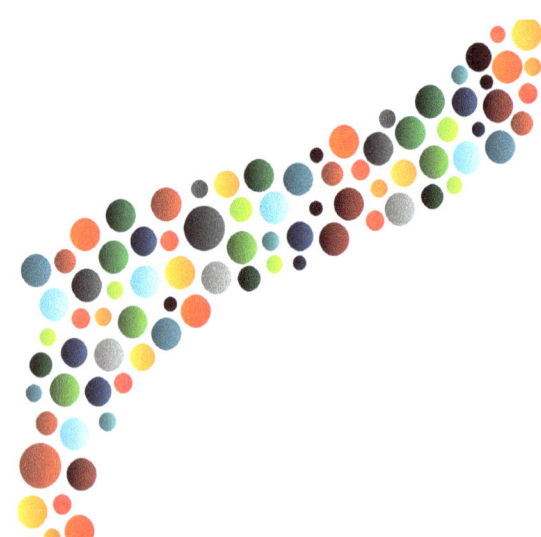

This Book can be used with:

The Coping Skills Workbook for Children
Adult Edition

Denise Folsom, MS, LMHC, RPT, NBCC

The Legacy House
thelegacyhousepc.org
denise@thelegacyhousepc.com

Interior Design: Denise Folsom, LMHC, RPT, NBCC
Self-publishing: Kristi Knowles

© 2020 Denise Folsom, LMHC, RPT, NBCC All Rights Reserved

No part of this publication may be reproduced, stored in a retrieval system, or transmitted in any form by any means - electronic, mechanical, photocopy, recording or otherwise - except for brief quotations in critical reviews or articles, without the prior permission of the author, except as provided by U.S. copyright law. Requests for permission should be addressed in writing to Denise@TheLegacyHousePC.com.

Paperback ISBN: 978-1-7369453-0-8

This is MY book

Decorate this page in any way you like.

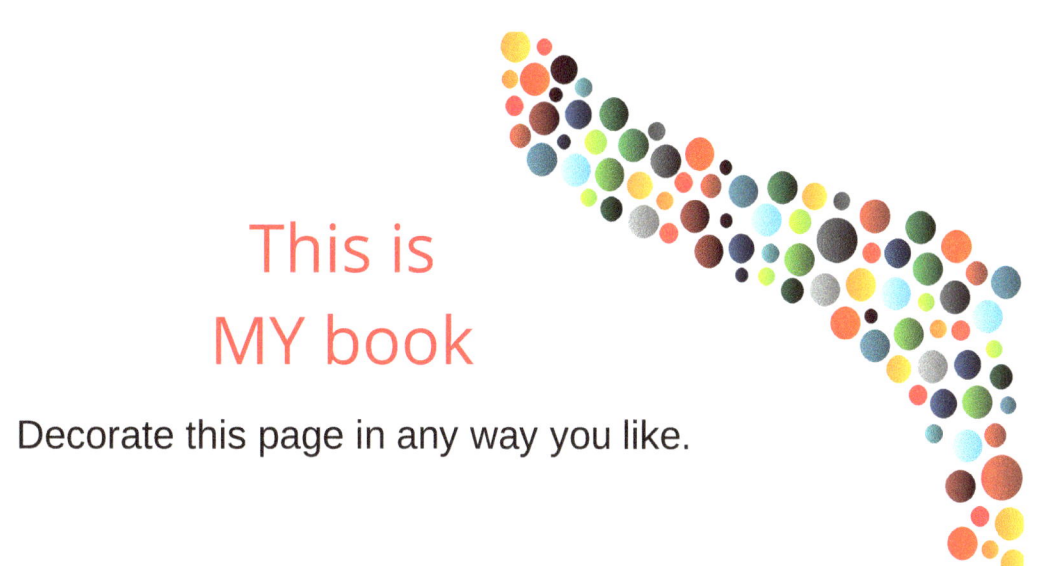

What are Coping Skills?

Coping skills are ways that you can think about a problem or actions you can do to help you with a problem. Coping skills can help you deal with difficult situation and emotions.

<u>Draw or write about the things that are hard for you.</u>
This might be something at school or at home. Maybe there is someone at your school who is mean. Maybe you have a hard time when it's time to stop playing or when it's time to go to bed.

What are my Emotions?

Emotions and feelings are the same thing. Sometimes you may act mad, but really you feel hurt because of what someone said. You may act happy, but you are sad inside. Here's a list of feeling words.

*happy   sad   afraid   surprised   mad   small
content   bugged   shy   glad   blah   annoyed
startled   curious   pleased   blue   irritated   playful
gloomy   mean   tense   weird   rotten   crabby   anxious
confused   cranky   worried   calm   unhappy   grumpy
empty   grouchy   timid   quiet   cozy   jealous   safe
embarrassed   relaxed   guilty   confident   strong   lonely
proud   great   loved   fed-up*

Choose a few of the words and then choose a marker or crayon that best fits the feeling. Write them below. I wrote one out for you as an example.

Angry

When do I act that way?

If you look at the feelings that you wrote out, you may find that you have some of the feelings when certain things happen. Example:

I get mad when someone calls me a name.

Can you match the feeling with what is happening when you feel that way? Let's try.

Feeling	What is happening
Mad	⟶ _____
Happy	⟶ _____
Excited	⟶ _____
Strong	⟶ _____
Shy	⟶ _____
Quiet	⟶ _____

What helps?

You may already have some things that help you when you are upset. Can you think of any?

Maybe you....count, walk away, play a game, talk to someone, watch a video, or listen to music. Think of anything you already do that makes you feel better and draw or write them below.

The next page will help you think of people who can help.

Resource Figures

Where is a place maybe you already have been, that you have seen in pictures, or a place that is only in your imagination, where you can feel safe or peaceful?

_____
_____
_____

Can you think of a time that made you feel good about yourself or made you feel like a grown up? A time that you did a good job or made a good decision.

_____
_____
_____

Who are the people in your life who care about you?

_____
_____
_____

When was a time that you felt like someone was on your side or had your back? A time when someone protected you or you protected someone else. Maybe it's an animal or a superhero that protected someone.

_____
_____
_____

Can you think about someone who is magical or has special powers?

_____
_____
_____

Think of these things as being part of a team that can help you when you are upset. How can each of these things or people help?

_____
_____
_____
_____

Kinds of Coping Skills

There are a bunch of different kinds of coping skills. We are going to try some out and see which ones you like. The kinds of coping skills that we are going to try are:

Calming

_____
_____
_____

Distracting

_____
_____
_____

Physical

_____
_____
_____

Processing

_____
_____
_____

Try the coping skills on the next few pages to see if they help. Keep track of them in the spaces above.

Calming Coping Skills

Imagining/Thinking

What's your favorite place? (Write or draw it here.)

Think of your favorite things. (Write or draw them here)

Calming Coping Skills

Imagining/Thinking

Name animals that are a certain color.
How many animals can you name that are black?
_____
_____
_____

How many animals can you name that are green?
_____
_____
_____

How many animals can you name that have three colors?
_____
_____
_____
_____

Name five soft animals.

1._____

2._____

3._____

4._____

5._____

Calming Coping Skills

Sensory-Based Coping Skills

Find something that you can squeeze.

Stress Ball

Modeling Clay

Fist Clench

Squeeze your hands into fists and hold them for ten seconds.
Release and repeat three times.
Shake them out.

Body Squeeze

Tense your whole body like a rock and hold this position for ten seconds. Release all your muscles. Repeat three times.

Calming Coping Skills

5, 4, 3, 2, 1
Take a few deep breaths.

Look
Look around for 5 things that you can see, and say them out loud.

Feel
Find 4 things that you can feel right now. Examples: Feet in shoes, hair on your neck, etc.

Listen
Stop, close your eyes and listen for 3 sounds.

Smell
Find 2 things that you can smell. You may have to get up and move.

Taste
Name 1 thing you can taste.
Example: Toothpaste from brushing your teeth. If you can't taste anything, name your favorite thing to taste.

Take a few deep breaths.

Calming Coping Skills

Moving/Action

Taste Test

List four favorite foods. Cut them into small pieces and then see if you can figure them out by taste only.

1._____
2._____
3._____
4._____

A Closer Look

Get a small rock or leaf. Look CLOSELY at it for 30 seconds. Use a magnifying glass if you have one. Look for things about the rock or leaf that you have never noticed before.

Draw the leaf/rock here. Make sure to draw the parts you did not notice before.

Cookie Breathing

Put a cookie in your hand and then bring it to your nose. Take a long, slow smell of the cookie. Talk about what you smell.

Pretend the cookie is warm and you need to cool it off before you eat it. Blow out a long, slow breath to cool off the cookie. Repeat smelling and cooling off the cookie three times.

Distraction Coping Skills

Thinking

<u>Imagine a trip.</u>

If you could go anywhere, where would you go?
_____
_____

Who would go with you?
_____
_____
_____

What would you need to take with you?
_____
_____
_____

<u>Counting</u>

- Count by 2's, 5's, 10's
- Count backward from 100 by 7's
- Count between 7 and 47 by 2's

Interacting

<u>Play a game</u>

List your favorite games here

1._____
2._____
3._____
4._____
5._____

<u>Playing</u>

- Play with pets or friends
- Play a video game

Distraction Coping Skills

Activity

List things that make you laugh (videos, movies, etc.)
_____
_____
_____
_____
_____

Talk a walk and notice new things in nature
Write the new things here. Gather leaves, sticks, etc. and make a mandala.

_____
_____
_____
_____
_____

Volunteer/Random act of kindness
Think of people/animals that you could do something nice for. Write their names here. Check them off as you do the nice thing.

✓ _____
___ _____
___ _____
___ _____

Physical Coping Skills

Dancing

List your favorite songs here. Make up a dance for each song.

_____
_____
_____
_____
_____

Exercise

Do each exercise and check them off when you finish.

_____ Do 5 jumping jacks
_____ Do 5 push ups
_____ Run in place for 30 seconds
_____ Touch your toes 10 times on each side
_____ Do 5 different stretches

Get Moving

- Play with building blocks
- Use a fidget toy
- Go for a swim
- Make an obstacle course
- Shred magazines/paper

Processing Coping Skills

Feeling thermometers

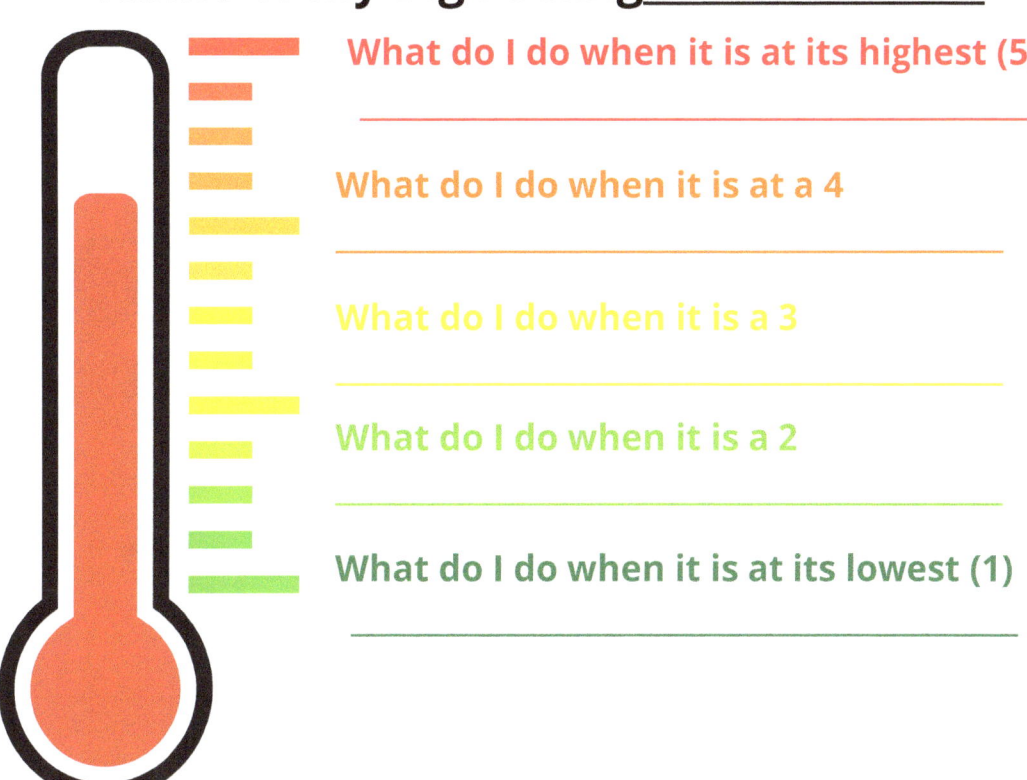

Get Creative
- Write in a journal
- Make a comic strip
- Make an anxiety box
- Create a music play list or video
- Write a letter or song

EMOTIONS

MAD

SAD

EXCITED

TIRED

LONELY

HAPPY

SCARED

LOVED

Here's the Plan

When I feel _____

_____

_____

_____

_____

What skills do you think you want to try?

1) _____

2) _____

3) _____

4) _____

5) _____

https://momentousinstitute.org/blog/upstairs-and-downstairs-brain

My Coping Skills

When I feel_____

I can_____

I can_____

Parent Check Off:

☐ WE DID IT!!!

☐ WE NEED MORE PRACTICE!!!

Notes: _____
_____
_____
_____

My Coping Skills

When I feel_____

I can_____

I can_____

Parent Check Off:

☐ WE DID IT!!!

☐ WE NEED MORE PRACTICE!!!

Notes: _____
_____
_____
_____

My Coping Skills

When I feel_____

I can_____

I can_____

Parent Check Off:

☐ WE DID IT!!!

☐ WE NEED MORE PRACTICE!!!

Notes: _____
_____
_____
_____

My Coping Skills

When I feel_____

I can_____

I can_____

Parent Check Off:

☐ WE DID IT!!!

☐ WE NEED MORE PRACTICE!!!

Notes: _____
_____
_____
_____

My Coping Skills

When I feel_____

I can_____

I can_____

Parent Check Off:

☐ WE DID IT!!!

☐ WE NEED MORE PRACTICE!!!

Notes: _____
_____
_____
_____

My Coping Skills

When I feel_____

I can_____

I can_____

Parent Check Off:

☐ WE DID IT!!!

☐ WE NEED MORE PRACTICE!!!

Notes: _____
_____
_____
_____

My Coping Skills

When I feel_____

I can_____

I can_____

Parent Check Off:

☐ WE DID IT!!!

☐ WE NEED MORE PRACTICE!!!

Notes: _____
_____
_____
_____

What worked for me:

When I felt _____

_____

_____

_____

_____

I used these skills:

1) _____

2) _____

3) _____

4) _____

5) _____

https://momentousinstitute.org/blog/upstairs-and-downstairs-brain

About the Author:

Denise Folsom, LMHC, RPT, NBCC

Denise Folsom, LMHC, RPT, NBCC, is a licensed mental health counselor in private practice in Panama City Florida.

Her specialties include attachment and trauma.

She works with clients of all ages, including very young children and active-duty military.

Denise is a registered play therapist, a licensing supervisor and a former educator, with extensive training in complex trauma and play therapy. She is certified in EMDR and does consultation work with other clinicians.

She is also the wife of a retired military member and mother of adult children.

www.ingramcontent.com/pod-product-compliance
Lightning Source LLC
Chambersburg PA
CBHW051304110526
44589CB00025B/2934